Rain

by Gail Saunders-Smith

Content Consultant:
Ken Barlow, Chief Meteorologist
KARE-TV, Minneapolis
Member, American Meteorological Society

Pebble Books
an imprint of Capstone Press

1

Pebble Books

Pebble Books are published by Capstone Press
818 North Willow Street, Mankato, Minnesota 56001
http://www.capstone-press.com

Library of Congress Cataloging-in-Publication Data
Saunders-Smith, Gail.
    Rain/by Gail Saunders-Smith.
        p. cm.
    Includes bibliographical references and index.
    Summary: Simply describes what rain is and the cycle that repeatedly brings water to the
earth.
    ISBN 1-56065-778-2
    1. Rain and rainfall—Juvenile literature. [1. Rain and rainfall. 2. Hydrological cycle.] I. Title.
QC924.7.S28 1998
551.57'7—dc21   98-5052
                                                                                  CIP
                                                                                   AC

Note to Parents and Teachers

This book describes and illustrates rain and the water cycle. The close picture-text matches support early readers in understanding the text. The text offers subtle challenges with compound and complex sentence structures. This book also introduces early readers to expository and content-specific vocabulary. The expository vocabulary is defined in the Words to Know section. Early readers may need assistance in reading some of these words. Readers also may need assistance in using the Table of Contents, Words to Know, Read More, Internet Sites, and Index/Word List sections of the book.

410 3080

Table of Contents

4

Rain is precipitation.
Precipitation is any kind of
water that falls from clouds.
Snow is precipitation, too.
Snow falls when tiny raindrops
turn into ice.

6

Rain brings water to all living things. Rain fills rivers and lakes. Animals like frogs need to live near water. Most animals need to drink water every day.

Rain goes into the ground. Grass and other plants use water in the ground. People dig wells into the ground to get water. People use water to drink, clean, and cook.

Rain starts as water on the ground. Water in oceans and lakes evaporates into the air. Evaporate means to turn into vapor. Vapor is tiny drops of water. The drops are so small they float in the air.

Water vapor rises high into the sky. The tiny drops get colder and stick to dust in the air. The water and dust form clouds. Clouds turn dark as the water drops grow bigger. Rain falls when the water drops are heavier than the air.

Rain is part of the water cycle. Water evaporates and makes clouds. Then rain falls from clouds. This happens again and again.

Floods happen when too much rain falls. Floods drown plants and hurt buildings. Flash floods happen when a lot of rain falls quickly. Flash floods can move houses, cars, and trees.

Droughts happen when too little rain falls. Rivers and lakes dry up. The soil becomes hard. Plants and animals can die without water to drink.

Too much or too little rain can kill living things. Plants, animals, and people need just enough rain.

Words to Know

cycle—when something happens over and over

drought—a long time without any rain

evaporate—when something wet goes into the air; when water evaporates, it turns into vapor

flood—when so much rain falls that the water covers the ground; rivers and lakes cannot hold all the water in a flood

precipitation—any kind of water that falls from clouds

soil—dirt or earth; plants grow in soil

vapor—tiny drops of water; the drops are small enough to float in the air

Read More

Grazzini, Francesca. *Rain Where Do You Come From?* Brooklyn, N.Y.:Kane/Miller Book Publishers, 1996.

Hiscock, Bruce. *The Big Storm.* New York: Atheneum, 1993.

Llewellyn, Claire. *Wind and Rain.* Hauppauge, N.Y.: Barron's, 1995.

Internet Sites

Athena, Earth and Space Science for K-12
http://inspire.ospi.wednet.edu:8001/index.html

Dan's Wild Wild Weather Page
http://www.whnt19.com/kidwx/index.html

Weather Dude
http://www.nwlink.com/~wxdude

Index/Word List

Word Count: 263
Early-Intervention Level: 12

Editorial Credits
Lois Wallentine, editor; Timothy Halldin, design; Michelle L. Norstad, photo research

Photo Credits
International Stock/John Michael, cover
Dwight Kuhn, 6
James P. Rowan, 12
Richard Hamilton Smith, 4, 10, 14
Unicorn Stock Photos/Sabrina Turner, 1; ChromoSohm/Sohm, 8; Aneal Vohra, 16; Martha McBride, 18; Marie Mills, 20

24